A PICTURE BOOK
OF
PASSOVER

by David A. Adler

illustrated by Linda Heller

HOLIDAY HOUSE
NEW YORK

To Caroline, Martin,
Shira, and Solomon

D. A.

To Sue

L. H.

Library of Congress Cataloging in Publication Data

Adler, David A.
A picture book of Passover.

Summary: Describes the events which led to the
liberation of the children of Israel from slavery in
Egypt, and explains some of the Passover traditions and
customs.

1. Passover—Juvenile literature. [1. Passover]
I. Heller, Linda, ill. II. Title.
BM695.P3A34   296.4'37   81-6983
ISBN 0-8234-0439-0   AACR2

The Story of Passover

The story of Passover is the story of a family that becomes a great nation. The family is Jacob's family. Jacob was also called Israel and his family was called the children of Israel.

The story begins with the Pharaoh, the ruler of Egypt.

One night the Pharaoh had two dreams. In the first, seven fat, healthy cows were eaten by seven thin, sickly cows. In the second dream, seven big ears of corn were eaten by seven small ears.

These dreams worried the Pharaoh. He asked his wise men to explain them to him, but they couldn't. Then the Pharaoh called in one of the children of Israel, the one who was living in Egypt. His name was Joseph.

"Both dreams are really one," Joseph explained. "With these dreams God has shown the Pharaoh what He is about to do. There will be seven good years followed by seven years when nothing will grow. You must save food during the seven good years for the seven years that follow."

The people did as Joseph advised. The food they saved, saved Egypt. And Joseph was honored and made a minister of the land. When Joseph's father and brothers and their families came to Egypt for food, they were honored too. There were seventy of them when they came. They settled in Goshen, a rich fertile section of Egypt.

Many years passed. Joseph, his father, and all Joseph's brothers died. The Pharaoh died too, and a new Pharaoh became the ruler of Egypt.

Now, there were no longer just seventy children of Israel living in Egypt. There were a great many more. When the new Pharaoh saw all those Israelites living in his country, he became worried. He was afraid that if there was a war the Israelites might join his enemies and fight against Egypt.

The Pharaoh had a plan to keep the Israelites from becoming a powerful enemy. He would make them his slaves.

"Go now," he told his advisors. "Announce to the children of Israel that I will pay them to make bricks and to build walls around the cities of Pithom and Raamses."

At first the people of Egypt worked with the Israelites. Then, one by one, the Egyptians became the Israelites' masters. The Pharaoh stopped paying the children of Israel, and they became his slaves.

As slaves, the Israelites were forced into hard labor.
Any slave who did not work hard enough was whipped,
beaten, and sometimes killed. But even as slaves the
Israelites had more and more children until it seemed that
all Egypt was filled with the children of Israel.

Then the Pharaoh's astrologers, people who study the stars to learn about the future, warned the Pharaoh. They told him that an Israelite boy would be born who would one day lead his people against Egypt.

The astrologers couldn't tell the Pharaoh which boy it would be, so the Pharaoh ordered that every newborn Israelite boy be thrown into the river and drowned.

The Egyptians kept careful records. They knew when each Israelite baby was expected. When the baby was due, the Egyptians came. If the baby was a boy, they took him from his mother and threw him in the river.

But one Israelite baby was saved.

The boy was born three months earlier than expected. His mother hid him until she knew the Egyptians would be coming. Then she made a tiny ark out of reeds, mud, and tar. She placed the boy in the ark and hid it in the bulrushes along the edge of the river. The boy's sister Miriam watched to see what would happen to him.

A princess, the daughter of the Pharaoh, found the ark and took it from the water. She brought the baby to the palace, named him Moses, and raised him as her own son.

When Miriam saw the princess take her brother, Miriam ran to her. "Should I get you someone to nurse and care for the baby?" Miriam asked.

"Yes," the princess answered, and the girl ran and got Moses's mother. So the baby's nurse was his own mother.

As Moses grew older he knew that he was an Israelite. It hurt him terribly to see his people suffer as slaves. And one day, when Moses saw an Egyptian beating an Israelite, he beat the Egyptian. In his anger, Moses struck him with such force that the Egyptian died.

Moses was afraid that the Pharaoh would find out about what he had done, so he ran off. He ran a great distance to the land of Midian. In Midian he married and worked as a shepherd.

One day, many years later, while Moses was watching his sheep, he saw a bush that seemed to be burning. There were flames, but the bush wasn't harmed. Then Moses heard a voice call to him from the midst of the bush.

"Moses, Moses."

"Yes, here I am."

It was God speaking to Moses. "I have heard the cries of My people," God said. "I will deliver them out of Egypt and you will be their leader."

So Moses and his brother Aaron went to the Pharaoh and asked him to let the slaves go free.

The Pharaoh refused. "Those slaves are already too lazy," he said. "They don't need to be free. They need more work."

And the Pharaoh made the slaves work even harder.

Moses asked the Pharaoh again to let the Israelites go free. If he didn't, Moses warned, all the waters of Egypt would turn to blood.

The Pharaoh refused to let the slaves go and the waters in the rivers, the sea, and even in the jars that Egyptians kept in their homes turned to blood. That was the first plague. There were ten.

When the blood became water again, the second plague came. Frogs covered the land. They were everywhere. They were in the Egyptians' fields, in their homes, their ovens, and even in their beds.

When the frogs were gone, the third plague came. Thick clouds of lice swarmed over the land. They attacked the Egyptians and their animals.

When the lice were gone, the fourth plague came. Wild animals suddenly appeared. Lions, bears, and wolves ran through Egypt, ruining whatever was in their way. But, like the other plagues, the animals did not attack the children of Israel.

When the animals were gone, the fifth plague came. A deadly disease attacked the Egyptian's cattle.

When the cattle stopped dying, the sixth plague came. Painful boils broke out on the skin of the Egyptians.

After each plague, the Pharaoh was given a chance to end the suffering by letting the slaves go free. But the Pharaoh always refused.

When the boils were gone, the seventh plague came. Huge hailstones mixed with fire fell on Egypt.

When the hail stopped falling, the eighth plague came. A swarm of locusts darkened the land.

They ate every plant, vegetable, and the leaves and fruit off every tree.

When the locusts were gone, when nothing green remained, the ninth plague came. It became as dark as night in the middle of the day. Egyptians could not see their neighbors. But for the children of Israel it was light.

When the darkness ended, the tenth plague came. The firstborn in every Egyptian house would die.

The Pharaoh was terrified. He was a firstborn son.
In the middle of the night, as the firstborns were dying
throughout Egypt, the Pharaoh called for Moses and

"Leave now," he said. "Go quickly before we all die."

The Israelites left that very night.

The next day, when the Egyptians and the Pharaoh saw that the slaves were gone, they cried out, "What have we done? Why have we let them go free?"

With an army, soldiers, horses, and chariots, they chased after the children of Israel.

When the Israelites saw them coming, they were frightened. The Red Sea was ahead of them. The Egyptians were behind them. There seemed to be no place to go.

"Lift up your rod," God told Moses. "Stretch your
hand out over the sea."

Moses lifted his rod and stretched his hand over the

sea, and the sea divided. There were two large walls of
water with dry land between them. The Israelites walked
through the water to the other side of the sea.

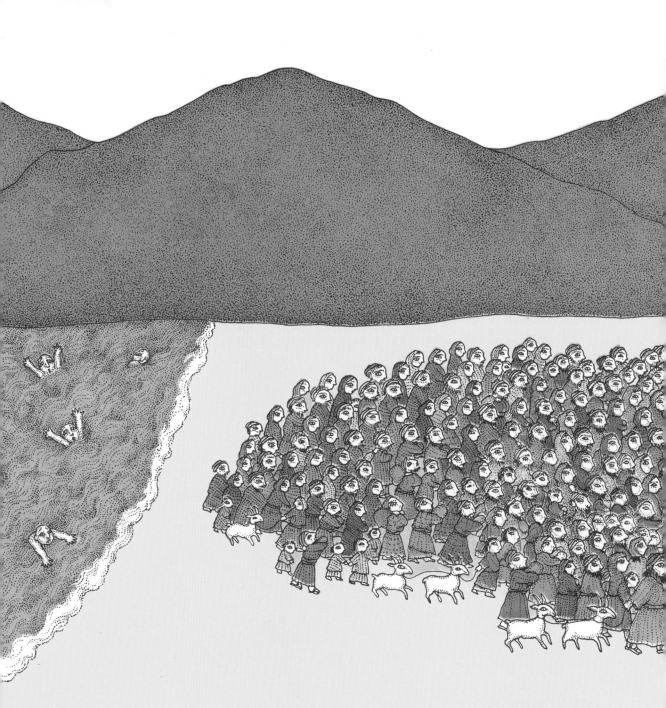

The Egyptians followed. When they were in the midst of the sea, Moses raised his hand again. The walls of water collapsed and flooded together. The Egyptians drowned. The Israelites were free.

When the Israelites came to Egypt, they were just seventy people. Now, standing at the edge of the sea, they were a huge free nation.

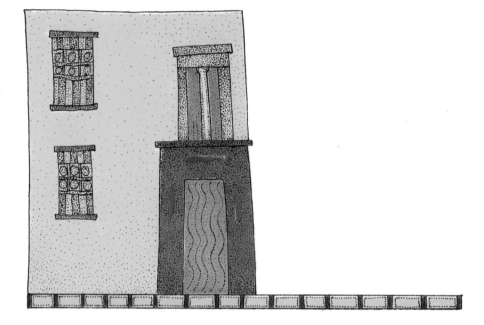

The Holiday of Passover

Passover, the name of the holiday celebrating our freedom, was taken from the tenth plague. When God sent the Angel of Death to the homes of the Egyptians to kill their firstborns, the angel "passed over" the homes of the Israelites.

Passover is also called *Hag ha-Abib,* the Spring Holiday, because that's when it's celebrated.

On the fourteenth night of Nisan, the Hebrew month which corresponds to March-April, there's a search for *hamez,* bread and other foods which are not allowed on Passover. We search our homes by candlelight.

Then, early the next morning, the *hamez* is burned. From then, until the end of Passover, no bread is eaten. And that night, the night of the fifteenth of Nisan, the holiday begins.

On the first night of Passover, and in traditional Jewish homes outside of Israel on the second night too, there is a special *seder* meal.

Near the beginning of the *seder* a short prayer, *Ha Lahma Anya,* is said. It sets the tone of the *seder*. The prayer announces that our homes are open to guests and that we wish to share what we have with others, especially the poor. The prayer ends with the hope that while this year there are slaves, next year we all hope to be free.

After the *Ha Lahma Anya,* a young child asks the Four Questions, the *Mah Nistannah.* The child wants to know why this night is different from all other nights. The answer, of course, is the story of Passover.

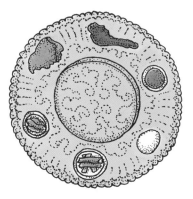

After the story has been told, we eat bitter herbs and remember the bitter taste of slavery.

We eat a clay-like paste called *haroset,* a mixture of apples, nuts, and wine. While we eat the *haroset,* we remember the clay the slaves used to make bricks.

We eat *matzah*, a flat kind of bread, and remember that the Israelites left Egypt so quickly, the bread they were baking didn't have a chance to rise. At the beginning of the seder, one piece of *matzah*, the *afikoman*, is hidden. Whoever finds it gets a prize.

During the seder we also drink wine, four cups of it. But we spill out some wine before we drink because our cups of wine and our happiness cannot be full when we remember that Egyptians died so that we could be free.